YOUR KNOWLEDGE

- We will publish your bachelor's and
  master's thesis, essays and papers

- Your own eBook and book -
  sold worldwide in all relevant shops

- Earn money with each sale

Upload your text at www.GRIN.com
and publish for free

Bibliographic information published by the German National Library:

The German National Library lists this publication in the National Bibliography; detailed bibliographic data are available on the Internet at http://dnb.dnb.de .

Imprint:

Copyright © 2015 GRIN Verlag, Open Publishing GmbH
Print and binding: Books on Demand GmbH, Norderstedt Germany
ISBN: 9783668336445

This book at GRIN:

http://www.grin.com/en/e-book/342671/fashion-specific-challenges-occurring-within-the-supply-chain-and-how-these

Lina Seil

Fashion specific challenges occurring within the supply chain and how these can be approached using Fast Fashion

Based on the example of the Spanish clothing retailer Zara

GRIN Publishing

GRIN - Your knowledge has value

Since its foundation in 1998, GRIN has specialized in publishing academic texts by students, college teachers and other academics as e-book and printed book. The website www.grin.com is an ideal platform for presenting term papers, final papers, scientific essays, dissertations and specialist books.

Visit us on the internet:

http://www.grin.com/

http://www.facebook.com/grincom

http://www.twitter.com/grin_com

Fashion specific challenges occurring within the supply chain and how these can be approached using Fast Fashion.

Based on the example of the Spanish clothing retailer Zara

Acadamic Paper

Fashion Management

submitted by

Lina Seil

Table of Contents

List of Abbreviations

CAD   Computer Aided Design

CAM   Computer Aided Manufacturing

CAP   Computer Aided Planning

CAQ   Compuer Aided Quality Assurance

EDI   Electronical Data Interchange

PDA   Personal Digital Assistants

PoS   Point of Sale

RFID   Radio-Frequency Identification

USP   Unique Selling Proposition

1. Introduction

1.1. Problems and Aims

"The faster people throw away their clothing, the sooner they buy something new – that's what keeps the wheel turning." That was Karl Lagerfeld's response in a recent interview when asked about the effect of Fast Fashion.[1]

But when discussing sustainability, the economic aspect cannot be ignored: in the short term, Fast Fashion invigorates the economy. Especially, the increasing sales numbers of H&M and Inditex[2] show that Fast Fashion seems to be a promising business model.

Fashion is changing faster and faster. Particularly in the last seasons the enormous rise in pace has been incomparable. Fashion bloggers post catwalk trends and street styles in real time and brands sell via social media. Referring to the fashion supply chain, the average fashion lead time, which starts at the design stage and ends with the finished product in stores, can seem like an eternity. It is near to impossible for a buyer to deter-mine which trend will be a bestseller in the next season. Nonetheless, while all competitors have to sell winter down jackets in July, Zara features new items twice per week in their stores. In the face of inconsistent weather, the pressure to manage footage in stores and changing consumer requirements, there are many challenges to deal with in the fashion supply chain.[3]

Generally, the fashion industrie's main supply chain challenges are the perishabilty of fashion goods, demand uncertainty and tight lead times. Due to that, the development and implementation of advanced supply chain strategies are becoming unavoidable. In the recent past a great variety of strategies emerged that may be an opportunity for all contigencies to proceed with these challenges and to gain a competitive advantage over their competitors. All strategies share the goal of increasing agility, flexibility and responsiveness. The most widespread supply chain strategy is Fast Fashion.[4]

The purpose of this chapter is to identify how fashion specific challenges, that occur within the supply chain, can be approached using Fast Fashion. Thereby, it will be explained what substrategies Fast Fashion consists of and how these can solve the problems of the fashion industry. Hereby, the focus is on strategic aspects of Supply Chain Management.

---

[1] Cf. Landowski (2015), p. 80
[2] Cf. Textilwirtschaft (2015): Das Ringen der Riesen, p. 20
[3] Cf. Landowski (2015), p. 80
[4] For further Information: Cf. Chopra (2013), p. 32 f.

1.2. Structure

First of all the focus of this academic paper lies on the conceptual fundamentals. This chapter will define and discuss the terms *Supply Chain, Supply Chain Challenges* and *Fast Fashion*. Secondly, the focus lies on the specific challenges of the fashion industry that occure within the supply chain: *Perishability, Demand Volatilty* and *Lead Times.* Then Fast Fashion and its sub topics - *Quick Response, Sourcing, Supply Chains* - will be explained in detail.

Following this, a case study of the Spanish fashion retailer Zara is presented to illustrate how Fast Fashion works in practice. This chapter is aimed at recognising how Fast Fashion approaches the fashion specific supply challenges de facto. At the beginning of this chapter, the company Zara will be introduced. Afterwards, a closer look is taken at how Fast Fashion works in practice based on the example of Zara.

Finally, the knowledge gained from the academic paper will be summarised in a con-clusion.

2. Conceptual Fundamentals

2.1. Definition Supply Chain

The term *Supply Chain* is fundamentally defined as a value-added process. This value-added process involves the transformation of natural resources, raw materials and components into a finished product that is delivered to the end customer. Due to this, it includes the production and service processes, distribution processes and marketing processes as well as transport and storage processes as sub-processes. Therefore, this concept follows the fundamental idea of the Value Chain of Porter.[5]

However, Porter's view is extended insofar, as the supply chain does not only include the company internal value-added processes, in which the scope of a supply chain is limited to one company, but also cross-company value-added processes. Moreover, the term supply chain is generally only used, if the value-added processes and steps are closely interlinked.[6] Furthermore, there are other normative concepts that also involve (process-) optimizations throughout the complete supply chain - for example in the form of inventory reductions throughout the entire process chain.[7]

According to this, a supply chain can generally be described as a system of organizations, people, activities, information, and resources involved in moving a product or service from supplier to customer. In a supply chain the corporate performance is governed by both value-

---

[5] Cf. Porter (2010), p. 25
[6] Cf. Hertel (2011), p. 6
[7] Cf. Liebmann (2008), p. 667

added and value-destroying factors such as design and image.[8]

Besides, the term supply chain is closely related to the concept of Value Chains. It is partly used in a similar context or even synonymous.[9]

Furthermore, supply chains are managed through *Supply Chain Management*. Supply chain management encompasses "the planning and management of all activities involved in sourcing and procurement, conversion, and all logistics management activities. Importantly, it also includes coordination and collaboration with channel partners, which can be suppliers, intermediaries, third-party service providers, and customers."[10] But due to limited scope the topic supply chain management will not be a central theme in this academic paper.

2.2. Definition Supply Chain Challenges

Over the past decades, the supply chain has become complex and vulnerable. Due to this, supply chain leaders have seen increasing challenges. They must address these challenges to create and remain efficient and effective supply chain methods. To get a quick overview of the main challenges occurring within the supply chain the most recent challenges are described in the following section.

One of these challenges is the *globalization of manufacturing operation*. Because of this it is important to have a global procurement network that can support and react to the supply chain's needs. Selecting a strategic supplier that provides manufacturing locations with consistent global quality and a reliable local service is a challenge.[11]

Moreover, *shorter lead times, less inventory and better throughput* also present current challenges. With shorter product life cycles and changing market demands, companies are forced to embark on a lean journey. It is important to note that the supply strategies in a lean environment support the operation's strategy. The challenge is always to find not just a lean concept, but a working lean solution.

Furthermore, a *supplier based consolidation* is another challenge that is often faced in a supply chain. Consolidation of the supply base can bring many advantages. It eliminates supply base variances and overheads. The challenge is to find a supplier with solutions and experience in supplier-based consolidation processes.

---

[8] Cf. Werner (2013), p. 18 f.
[9] Cf. Hertel (2011), p. 6
[10] Cf. Candian Supply Chain Sector Council (2015): Supply Chain Definitions, p. 1
[11] Cf. Swartz, Inbound Logistics (N. D.): Challenges for Today's Global Supply Chains, p. 1

And finally, *access to the latest technology* in various fields by having the right experts has proven to be a great support in product development. It is a challenge to earn the latest know-how in technology.[12]

Especially, fashion supply chains' main challenges are the *Pershiabilty* of fashion products, the *Demand Uncertainty* that is difficult to assess and the long *Lead Times*. These challenges will be discussed in detail in the following chapter of this academic paper.

2.3. Definition Fast Fashion

Fast Fashion is a contemporary term used by fashion retailers to explain that designs are quickly captured from the catwalk in order to create current fashion trends – in technical language this is called the fast follower or copy-cat behavior.[13] So, Fast Fashion refers to the rapid copying of catwalk designs and the most recent fashion trends presented at fashion shows in both the spring and the autumn of every year for clothing collections.[14]

Moreover, Fast Fashion emphasizes on optimizing certain aspects of the supply chain in order to design and manufacture quickly.[15]

Spanish fashion retailer Zara has been at the forefront of this fashion retail revolution and their brand has almost become synonymous with the term.[16]

Nowadays, the philosophy of quick manufacturing at an affordable price is used in large retailers such as H&M, Asos, Forever21 and Topshop. They offer the latest models of famous designers and celebrities at significant lower prices according to the concept of Quick-Response within a few weeks. By now, six to eight new collections within one year are quite common. Fast Fashion is connected to the higher number of (sub-) collections and delivery dates. This implies that the preliminary lead time for the production no longer needs numerous months, but rather just a few weeks. Therefore, entrepreneurs are forced to provide the materials in advance and to produce closer to the market or take expensive transport routes. This also means that bestsellers from a range can be reproduced in a short time and that simple styles are sometimes offered in new colours.

According to the Greenpeace study "Toxic yarns. The large textile-testing by Green-peace", Zara is the leading Fast Fashion brand. The retailer can put together a line of clothing within seven to 30 days and deliver bestsellers in addition within only five days to the stores.

---

[12] Cf. Bossard Proven Productivity (2015): Supply Chain Management – Challenges and Solutions, p. 1 f.
[13] Cf. Lexikon der Nachhaltigkeit (2015): Fast Fashion, p. 1
[14] Cf. Hines (2007), p. 40
[15] Cf. Textilwirtschaft (2013): Das Ringen der Riesen, p. 20 ff.
[16] Cf. Zentes (2011), p. 274

By now, even luxury brands like Chanel and Louis Vuitton join the Fast Fashion trend. They try to be perceived as relevant and current with additional collections – another result of the Fast Fashion industry.[17]

Fast Fashion is also in contrast to the current Slow Fashion movement that supports sustainable, conscious and decelerated fashion, as well as a fair production.[18] The Slow Fashion movement has arisen in opposition to Fast Fashion, blaming it for pollution (both in the production of clothes and in the decay of synthetic fabrics), poor workmanship, and focusing on very brief trends rather than classic style. Fast Fashion has also come under criticism because suppliers are forced to comply with increasingly tight delivery dates due to the production pressure and thereby wage cuts, irresponsible practices and poor working conditions in developing countries are more apparent.[19]

3. Fashion Specific Challenges

The textile retail faces many supply chain challenges. This section focuses on the main fashion specific challenges: Perishability, Demand Uncertainty and Lead Times.

3.1. Perishability

The term "Fashion" is defined "as a broad term that typically encompasses any market or product where there is an element of style which is likely to be shortlived." (Christoper et. al., 2004, p. 367) The advantage of a fashion product over an ordinary commodity lies within its novelty and exclusiveness. This advantage only exists as long as the product corresponds to the latest trend and has certain uniqueness.[20] This means that the demand is not already saturated by price reductions. So, if the specific advantage is lost, the item can only be sold for a substantially lower price.[21] Therefore perishable products, like fashion products, are less likely to sell over time due to seasonal changes in fabric-ation, style and color.[22]

Fashion also moves in cycles, which is decisive for the success of a product.[23] In general, there are two types of products with limited lifecycles differentiated: "Fashion" and "Seasonal". Fashion products have lifecycles of approximately 10 weeks, while seasonal products have lifecycles of approximately 20 weeks.[24]

---

[17] Cf. Lexikon der Nachhaltigkeit (2015): Fast Fashion, p. 1
[18] Cf. Choi (2014), p. 13
[19] Cf. Lexikon der Nachhaltigkeit (2015): Fast Fashion, p. 1
[20] For further Information: Cf. Easey (2009), p. 149 f.
[21] Cf. Barnes (2006), p. 283
[22] Cf. Donnellan (2014), p. 188
[23] For further Information: Cf. Textile Learner (N. D.): Fashion Cyle – Steps of Fashion Cycles, p. 1 f.
[24] Cf. Fernie (2014), Fig. 6. 3., p. 126

Moreover, the traditional calendar year is divided into two distinctive periods: Spring/ Summer and Autumn/Winter.[25] The seasonal key fashion trends are presented at fashion shows, trade fairs and fabric events more than half a year before the particular season begins.[26] The design departments of apparel companies transfer these trends into mass-market products. However, at the present time, the calendar year is diverged in twelve sub-seasons – instead in the two traditional seasons. Along with the transformation of the common seasons Spring/Summer and Autumn/Winter, the importance of high-end fashion shows declines. Thereby, more and more inter-seasonal shows are launched. These are often more commercial than the traditional ones, because they normally show fashion trends, which are closer to the mass-market.[27]

Further, social media and its prevalence play an important role. Everybody can start their own fashion blog and reach an unlimited audience. The latest styles are exchanged all over the world in real time via Instagram and co. and reach the remotest places without any delay.[28]

Music, film, television, and other media also have great influence on fashion trends. Today's fashion trends are not defined twice a year, but can be created any time by any one. As soon as the corresponding products are on the market, the older ones become obsolete and lose their value-advantage.[29]

The erosion of pre-defined product life cycles makes it much more difficult to estimate the point in time in which a certain product will perish. Thus in consumption, perishability is one of the main challenges a company has to face when dealing with fashion supply chains.

3.2. Demand Uncertainty

As the term fashion is defined as "as a broad term that typically encompasses any market or product where there is an element of style which is likely to be shortlived." (Christoper et. al., 2004, p. 367), it is implied that a fashion product is likely to be volatile, rapidly changing and hard to predict.[30] That means that sales data and empirical values about the demand of a fashion product do not exist. Thus, solid demand and sales forecasts are virtually impossible. Moreover, as customer's demands change faster these days, demand forcasting gets even harder.[31]

---

[25] Cf. Jackson (2006), p. 49
[26] Cf. Barnes (2006), p. 261
[27] Cf. Jackson (2006), p. 49 f.
[28] Cf. Landowski (2015), p. 80
[29] Cf. Barnes (2006), p. 261
[30] Cf. Barnes (2006), p. 283
[31] Cf. Jackson (2006), p. 100

The apparel industry has to deal with demand volatility coupled with enormously low predictability of demand.[32] Demand volatility generally means that "the ratio between stock-holding and return becomes more critical, needing a much faster response time to ensure that lower overall stock level are kept in stock at all times."[33]

Demand uncertainty is constituted as one of the most significant cost factors for fashion retailers. For clarification: Underrated demand leads to lost sales and unsatisfied customers. Especially because a high level of impulse buying, lost sales are very problematic.[34] Further, overrated demand causes excess stock. As fashion products are perishable, they lose value if they do not correspond to the latest trends and do not have uniqueness. Hence, the excess stock can only be sold for a substantially lower price.

Generally it can be said that massive costs occur because of demand misjudgement. In literature it is estimated that a huge percentage of all fashion products have to be sold at a marked down price. According to Sull and Turconi the industry average markdown ratio is about 50 per cent.[35]

Moreover, fashion sales are influenced by a variety of extrinsic factors that are unpredictable. Especially music, film, celebrities and other media have great influence on demand.[36] Hence, it is also difficult to forecast the developement of demand. Furthermore, the perishability of fashion products[37] and new trends occuring at all times increase demand uncertainity.[38] In consumption, it is necessary to adjust fashion supply chains in order to to deal with the challenge of demand uncertainty.

3.3. Lead Times

Shorter product lifecycles and rapidly changing consumer demands have led to a renewed focus on lead times.[39] Especially, because flexibility and responsiveness are crucial in fashion markets with unpredictable demand und perishable products, lead times play an important role.[40] Thereby, fashion retailers are faced with lead time competitions. These are characterised by three dimensions that must be managed effectively:

- „Time to market": Speed at which a new product can be brought to market
- „Time to serve": Speed at which a costumer's order can be served

---

[32] Cf. Barnes (2006), p. 272
[33] Jackson (2006), p. 100 f.
[34] Cf. Barnes (2006), p. 272
[35] Cf. Choi (2014), p. 10
[36] Cf. Barnes (2006), p. 261
[37] Cf. Barnes (2006), p. 283
[38] Cf. Landowski (2015), p. 80
[39] Cf. Fernie (2014), p. 82
[40] Cf. Fernie (2014), p. 84

- „Time to react": Speed at which the product range can be adjusted to a volatile demand.[41]

In general the term "lead time" is defined as the „gap between when an order is placed and when it is received".

As an example, there is generally the risk that a retailer misinterpretes a random increase in demand as a growing trend. If the retailer faces a lead time of two months, it will incorporate into its order the anticipated growth over two months when placing the order. In contrast, if the retailer faces a lead time of two weeks, it will incorporate the anticipated growth over two weeks (which will be much less). The same applies when a decrease in demand is interpreted as a declining trend.[42] This shows, if lead times are too long, such that a fashion retailer offers products to the market when its attractiveness is weaking, this may result in discounted stock and therefore less profit.[43]

In addtition, if a company produces in East Asia, it has to face lead times of around 20 to 29 weeks. In consideration of lifecycles for fashion products of 10 weeks and for seasonal products of 20 weeks, retailers have to plan their range of items well in advance for the next seasons. And as fashion products are perishable, competitive retailers with shorter lead times have the advantage to sell the latest trends much earlier. Thereby they can sell the products at a very profitable price as they have exclusivity.[44]

Especially in the past years, there was a massive shift of textile and clothing manu-facturing towards East Asian low-wage countries. Labour costs are much lower there - compared to low-wage markets as Turkey, Mexico, and Marocco. China became the biggest exporter in the clothing industry. But since the production is placed in East Asia, additional costs for logistics and inventory, caused by greater geographical distance, has increased. Further, the production in East Asia is marked by higher lead times incurred by a greater distance, lower productivity and inflexibility.[45]

In general, it points out, that the factor "speed" is crucial in the clothing industry. Its importance grows with the high perishability and increased demand uncertainty of fashion products.

3.4. Conclusion

The fashion supply chain faces three main challenges: Perishabilty, Demand Uncertianty, and Lead Times.

---

[41] Cf. Zentes (2012), p. 133
[42] Cf. Chopra (2013), p. 268
[43] Cf. Barnes (2006), p. 283
[44] Cf. Fernie (2014), Fig. 6. 3., p. 126
[45] Cf. Zentes (2011), p. 281 f.

Apparel retailers have to decide well in advance which products are expected to correspond to future trends and thus should be offered for future seasons.[46] But fashion products are highly perishable, as trends often only last a few weeks.[47] Only if a product is exclusively sold, the price maximum can be gained.[48] But a solid method to forecast the constumer's actual demand does not exist.[49] As a consequence of misjudged consumer demand, stock excess that is highly perishable increases. In contrast, stock shortages cause lost sales and dissatisfy costumers. Additionally, if lead times are too long, a fashion retailer will have its products available only when its attractiveness has already weakened. As a result, stock is discounted and, thus, less profit is generated.[50] All in all, the fashion specific challenges compound each other.

To face the specific challenges and to adjust the fashion supply chain, an advanced approach is needed. Thereby, the next section focuses on Fast Fashion.

4. Fast Fashion

Based on the chapter about the conceptual fundamentals previously, Cachon and Swinney define Fast Fashion as a "system (that) combines quick response production capabilities with enhanced product design capabilities to both design 'hot' products that capture the latest consumer trends and exploit minimal production lead times to match supply with uncertain demand."[51]

Fast Fashion's main elements are the concept of Quick Response, Enhanced Design, Responsiveness, and Sourcing and Agile Supply Chains. In the following sections the elements of Fast Fashion and how this system can improve the fashion supply chain will be discussed.

4.1. Quick Response

Quick Response stands for partnership-oriented systems between manufacturers and retailers that are aimed at speeding up the flow of goods. The concept of Quick Response is one of the first approaches to need-based control of goods and information flow. This is especially significant for fast demand changes. Both the diversity of variants in the fashion industry as well as the seasonal circumstances within the context of fashion collections form the basis of the Quick Response concept. The objective is to strongly couple the flow of goods through smaller order quantities and shorter or faster order cycles with the actual

---

[46] Cf. Diruf (2007), p. 7
[47] Cf. Donnellan (2014), p. 188
[48] Cf. Barnes (2006), p. 283
[49] Cf. Jackson (2006), p. 100
[50] Cf. Barnes (2006), p. 283
[51] Cachon and Swinney (2011), p. 778

demand. This increases the responsiveness to unforeseen changes (e. g. changes in fashion trends). Quick Response can be described as a supply chain strategy that focuses on flexibility and demand-driven supply.

Moreover, the Quick Response concept is based on article-precise registration of the sales data at the Point of Sale (PoS), which are regularly transmitted to the manufacturer. The production planning and control is also made on the basis of the sales data.[52]

The main components of Quick Response - concluded from several literature - Inventory Control, Product Planning and Barcoding / RFID are described below.

Inventory Control

Inventory Control helps optimizing order processing and fulfillment by reducing the amount of inventory it holds by ordering more frequently and in lower quantity. So Inventory Control is a set of actions that reduces lead times and inventory size in the supply chain. By replenishing stock, Inventory Control also helps to reduce inventory costs to minimize the space required for storage and to better match with market conditions.[53] From there, it is particularly important that the right level of inventory is defined through Inventory Control. Because on the one hand, high levels improve responsiveness but also leave the supply chain vulnerable to the need for markdowns. On the other hand, low levels improve inventory turns but may result in lost sales if the costumer demand is not met correctly.[54] Keeping inventory low is especially important, when dealing with fashion products, because they lose their value quickly due to the perishabilty of fashion.[55]

In consumption, Inventory Control is characterized by short production cycles, high turnover rates, small orders and reduced waiting time.

Product Planning

Product Planning is supported by several technologies - for example Computer Aided Planning (CAP) to create work schedules, Computer Aided Manufacturing (CAM) to control the manufacturing processes and and Compuer Aided Quality Assurance (CAQ) to foster preventative quality management.[56] Especially Computer Aided Design (CAD) is used most commonly. [57]

CAD is defined as a „production technolgy in which computers perform new product design."[58] It has two areas of activity - design and detailing. The focus of the design is on

---

[52] Cf. Zentes (2012), p. 603
[53] Cf. Berman (2013), p. 418
[54] Cf. Chopra (2013), p. 59
[55] Cf. Draft (2010), p. 819
[56] For further Details: Cf. Werner (2013), p. 297 ff.
[57] Cf. Werner (2013), p. 300 f.
[58] Cf. Draft (2010), p. 817

calculations and the creation of manufacturing documents. [59] A draft can be modelled and analysed digitally – this allows optimizing the designed product from the very beginning. Therefore, CAD helps performing design operations in about half the time required with traditional methods.[60] In detail, an ideal combination is tried to be selected from the multitude of alternatives. The drafts of the design are complemented by technical information (materials, surfaces, etc.) and the part numbers for each product shall be deposited in parts lists. All in all, CAD is the interface between designs and manufacturing that helps reducing lead times.[61]

Electronical Data Interchange (EDI)

Many technologies exist to share and analyze information throughout the supply chain. One common technology is *Electronic Data Interchange.*[62]

It is defined as a "paperless, computer-to-comptuer relationship between retailers and vendors."[63] EDI stands for the cross-company transmission of structured and standardized business or the transaction information between participating companies using open electronic communication methods. Thus, structured business processes can be sup-ported by EDI.[64] Due to EDI retailers and suppliers regularly exchange information with regards to inventory levels, delivery times, unit sales etc. As a result, both sides enhance their decision-making capabilities, better control inventory and are more responsive to demand. Every stage of the fulfillment cycle is reliant on accurate and timely information being passed on electronically.[65] Due to this, EDI makes transactions faster and more accurate.[66] Thereby, lead times can be effectivly shortened.[67] Moreover, EDI lets retailers do QR inventory planning efficiently.[68] Furthermore, by the use of EDI supply chains flow more smoothly. And improving the timing and accuracy in the delivery of products, relationships with customers and vendors are strengthened.[69]

Barcoding and Radio-Frequency Identification (RFID)

To compass Quick Response, it is particularly important to obtain information on all digital material flows and sites throughout the supply chain. This is possible using barcodes or RFID chips. All units of a supply chain can be equipped with a barcode or RFID that identifies them. Using barcode information - about all types of stock in all points of the supply chain -

[59] Cf. Werner (2013), p. 300 f.
[60] Cf. Draft (2010), p 817
[61] Cf. Werner (2013), p. 300 f.
[62] Cf. Chopra (2013), p. 65
[63] Cf. Berman (2013), p. 419
[64] Cf. Zentes (2012), p. 615
[65] Cf. Berman (2013), p. 236
[66] Cf. Chopra (2013), p. 65
[67] Cf. Donnellan (2006), p. 342
[68] Cf. Berman (2013), p. 419
[69] Cf. Berman (2013), p. 236

can be entered in a central data system.[70] An emerging alternative to *Barcoding* is *Radio-Frequency Identification* technology. Information is fed into the central data system by using radio transmitters instead of barcodes.[71] It serves a similar purpose as Barcoding, but in fashion supply chains RFID has significantly higher performance, automation and capability. In conjunction with an EDI system or CAD system, digital information is stored in barcodes or RFID chips in real time across the entire chain and can be made available. This can improve the material flow enormously - lead times are reduced and responsiveness is improved. Incoming shipments can be scanned, checked against purchase orders and paid immediately.[72]

4.2. Sourcing: Responsiveness and Efficiency

The fashion industry has been facing one specific challenge regarding supply chain management for several years: Sourcing. Therefore, it is not only important to supply stores with the lowest possible amount at the beginning of the season and to satisfy the demand of products that are identified as sales-promoting through replenishment systems. It is also important to perform as many collections changes in the shortest possible time within the season. This requires fast response times on latest fashion trends. Fast post-production on the basis of sales data and production, which is located near to the market, acts as a suitable solution.[73]

For this reason the production location is one of the most important factors of the fashion supply chain. Decisions regarding the location, capacity and flexibilities of facilities have a significant impact on the supply chain's performance. Responsiveness and efficiency play an important role in the discussion about the production location. Therefore, the aim is to achieve a high level of responsiveness at the lowest possible cost.[74]

Especially sourcing decisions[75] affect both the responsiveness and efficiency of a supply chain. For example, sourcing in low-wage countries like China allows a firm to increase efficiency by providing its products at low costs while responsiveness suffers due to the long distance to the market.[76]

---

[70] Cf. Werner (2013), p. 285
[71] For further Information: Cf. Werner (2013), p. 286 ff.
[72] Cf. Chopra (2013), p. 65
[73] Cf. Zentes (2012), p. 608
[74] Cf. Chopra (2013), p. 53
[75] „Purchasing, also called procurement, is the process by which companies acquire raw materials, components, products, services, or other resources from suppliers to execute their operations. Sourcing ist he entire set of business processes required to purchase goods and services." Cf. Chopra (2013), p. 440
[76] Cf. Chopra (2013), p. 54

The key sourcing decision for a company is whether to produce in-house or outsource it to a third-party. Outsourcing means that a third party performs the supply chain function.[77] Moreover, a firm has to decide if all production processes should be outsourced, the responsive component should only be outsourced, or only the efficient component should be outsourced. The decision should be driven in part by the impact on the whole supply chain. So, outsourcing makes good economic sense, if the third partner raises the surplus more[78] as the company itself can. The growth in surplus results from aggregating capa-city, inventory, transportation, warehousing, procurement, and information to a level that a corporation cannot do on its own.[79] On the contrary, a corporation keeps the production in-house if the third partner cannot increase the surplus or if the risk[80] contigent on outsourcing is substainable.[81] Companies can also offshore its production - then the firms maintain the ownership of the facilities.[82]

In general, a company either follows the strategy to source in a local and domestic country with high labour costs nearby the market like Germany. Or a company sources in a nearby low-wage country like Morocco. A firm can also source offshore in an East Asian country with low wages.[83]

As mentioned above, sourcing decisions directly impact costs. However, it also takes effect on the quality, inventories, and inbound transportations costs.[84] All in all, sourcing decisions should be made to increase the surplus that is shared across the supply chain. The surplus is affected by costs such as production costs, inventory costs, and transportations costs.[85]

Due to this, in the context of Fast Fashion, sourcing takes place geographically and logistically close to the market in a nearby low-wage country. As a result, there is a return of manufacturing from East Asia back to regions close to the main fashion markets. However, this is accompanied by higher labour costs.[86] The competitive advantage of this speed-sourcing concept is particularly in the rapid response to latest fashion trends as the demanded products can be transported to the stores in much less time.[87]

Moreover, the product types play an important role within the context of sourcing decisions for apparel. It is economically reasonable to source basic apparel with long life cycles and stable, well-known demand offshore in East Asia. In contrast, fashion products have short life

---

[77] Cf. Chopra (2013), p. 440
[78] For further Information: Cf. Chopra (2013), p. 446 f.
[79] Cf. Chopra (2013), p. 446
[80] For further Information: Cf. Chopra (2013), p. 447 f.
[81] Cf. Chopra (2013), p. 68
[82] Cf. Chopra (2013), p. 441
[83] Cf. Hines (2007), p. 57 f.
[84] Cf. Chopra (2013), p. 67
[85] Cf. Chopra (2013), p. 66
[86] Cf. Fernie (2014) , p. 84
[87] Cf. Zentes (2012), p. 608

cycles and volatile demand. For fashion products, it is advisable to source locally to satisfy short-term demand and to increase flexibility. These advantages surpass the higher manufacturing costs.[88] Hence, a reasonable strategy could be a mixed sourcing strategy. This is where the demanded basic products are sourced from offshore, while additional demanded fashion products are sourced in quick local sources.[89]

This proves to be true by considering that Zara, one of the most responsive and successful Fast Fashion retailers, produces 27% of its goods in East Asia[90]. So, it is advisable trying to make the production facilities in high-cost locations very responsive and while keeping its facilities in low-cost countries efficient.[91]

4.3. Supply Chains

Supply chains are central to the creation of Fast Fashion. As described in the chapter of the conceptual fundamentals, supply chain systems are designed to reduce costs and to add value in the process of moving goods from design concept to retail stores and finally through to consumption. There are two kinds of supply chains, agile and lean. [92]

Agile and Lean Supply Chains

Agile Supply Chains are defined as short, flexible, demand driven supply chains - oppossed to traditional supply chain concepts like Lean Supply Chains that are forcast driven and characterized by high levels of inventory.[93] "Leanness" implies a stock-minimizing approach. So, a Lean Supply Chain is characterized as the correct appro-priation of the commodity for the product Due to that, Lean Supply Chains are better used, when large quanitites are produced and when there is less variability in a more stable environment. But Lean Supply Chains are not optimal for certain product types such as fashion and the principle of agility should be taken as a target for successful supply chains there.[94]

Agile Supply Chains are characterized by market sensitive, virtual, process integration, and network based.[95] The key factor of Agile Chains is, that they are driven by the latest information from both market and supplier side (e. g. market data from the point of sale). This allows Agile Supply Chains to become more responsive to changes in demand in the market

---

[88] Cf. Hines (2007), p. 57
[89] Cf. Chopra (2013), p. 54
[90] Cf. Zentes (2012), p. 704
[91] Cf. Chopra (2013), p. 54
[92] Cf. Barnes (2006), p. 264
[93] Cf. Barnes (2006), p. 264
[94] Cf. Zentes (2012), p. 709
[95] Cf. Zentes (2012), Abb. 5.69, p. 709

place. For example, information from the PoS can be used across the supply chain for immediate ordering and replenishment decisions. [96]

Leagile Supply Chains

Agile and Lean Supply Chains follow a very different approach, but that does not mean they cannot be combined. It is possible to design a supply chain that joins the advantages of each strategy and is both lean and agile. The combination of Agile and Lean Supply Chains is called *Leagile Supply Chains*.[97]

Basically, mass-market fashion products are characterized by the same basic elements. These are further modified and combined to produce the final unique product. Therefore, it is reasonable to devide the fashion supply chain into two sections: On the one hand, a lean, more cost-effective part, where the product is a commodity with little variety and constant demand. On the other hand, an agile part where the product is advanced to a specific fashion product with volatile demand.[98] Gatorina et al. describe such systems as "Leagile", "a combination of lean and agile approaches combined at the decoupling point for optimal supply chain management."[99] The point where the supply chain shifts from the forward-planned lean part to the market-driven agile part is called "decoupling point". It "seperates the custumer-order part of the activities [...] from the activities that are based on forecasting and planning."[100]

4.4. Conclusion

This chapter illustrates how Fast Fashion sets challenges towards the supply chain within the fashion business. Thereby, responsiveness is the key term behind Fast Fashion.

Especially Quick Response offers a great variety of possibilities to achieve responsive-ness. For example, sharing information steadily increases responsiveness and market visibility for the manufacturing processes.[101] Also other parts of the supply chain like designers, profit from an uninhibited flow of information. Designers use sales data in real time and respond quickly to consumer demand.[102] Through the use of information and communication technology such as CAD or EDI, lead times can be shortened.[103] Regarding Sourcing, a mixed strategy based on the concept of sourcing basic products from offshore, while sourcing fashion products in quick local sources proves to be reasonable.[104] Further, an Agile

---

[96] Cf. Barnes (2006), p. 264
[97] Cf. Lamb (2010), p. 462
[98] Cf. Lamb (2010), p. 462
[99] Cf. Tandler (2013), Tab. 3. 4., p. 174
[100] Cf. Tandler (2013), p. 176
[101] Cf. Berman (2013), p. 418
[102] Cf. Draft (2010), p. 817
[103] Cf. Chopra (2013), p. 65
[104] Cf. Chopra (2013), p. 54

and Leagile Supply Chain with both responsiveness and cost efficiency should be developed and implemented by a Fast Fashion company.[105]

In the following chapter the important factors of Fast Fashion will be desribed in detail by a case study about the Spanish Fast Fashion retailer Zara.

5. Zara - Fast Fashion in Practice

5.1. The Company

Zara is a Spanish clothing and accessories retailer based in Arteixo, Galicia, and founded in 1975 by Amancio Ortega and Rosalía Mera. It is the main brand of the Spanish Inditex Corporation (Industria de Diseño Textil, S.A).[106]

Inditex is a multinational clothing company and the world's largest apparel retailer. The fashion group operates over 6,460 stores stores worldwide[107] and owns further brands such as Massimo Dutti, Bershka, Pull and Bear, Uterqüe, Stradivarius and Oysho in several price segments.[108] The majority of its stores are company-managed.[109]

The first Zara shop opened in 1975 selling low price imitations of more up market fashion houses.[110] Currently, Zara has over 2000 stores strategically located in leading cities across 88 countries.[111] Zara's product ranges from women's wear to men's wear to children's wear.[112]

At the end of 2013, Inditex had sales of $16.7 billion[113] - for example compared to H&M with $20.2 billion and Mango with $2.1 bililon. Furthermore, Inditex sales increased by 8% - much stronger than its competitors.[114]

Zara has an almost complete vertical integration with optimization and high control of the supply chain in order to achieve a very high response rate to customer needs. Therefore, *time* is the most important factor, even more important than the production costs. Vertical integration enables shorter delivery times and offers high flexibility, so that the inventories and the fashion risk are minimized.[115]

Moreover, it is claimed that Zara needs just two weeks to develop a new product and to get it to stores, compared to the six-month industry average, and launches around 12,000 new

---

[105] Cf. Lamb (2010), p. 462
[106] Cf. Inditex (2015): Our History, p. 1
[107] Cf. Inditex (2015): Inditex at a Glace, p. 1
[108] For further Information: Cf. Zentes (2012), Tab. 5.3., p. 701
[109] For further Information: Cf. Zentes (2012), p. 701
[110] Cf. Inditex (2015): Our History, p. 1
[111] Cf. Inditex (2015): Zara, p. 1
[112] Cf. Forbes (2015): Zara Leads in Fast Fashion, p. 1
[113] Cf. Inditex Annual Report (2013), p. 3
[114] Cf. Forbes (2015): Zara Leads in Fast Fashion, p. 1
[115] Cf. Zentes (2012), p. 700

designs each year.[116] A very unusual strategy was its policy of zero advertising. The company preferred to invest a percentage of revenues in opening new stores instead. This has increased the idea of Zara as a "fashion imitator" company and low cost products.[117] Generally, Zara is known as one of the global market leaders in the fashion industry. It is also regarded as one of the most radical champions of the Fast Fashion concept.[118]

5.2. Fast Fashion in Practice

5.2.1. Business Model: Integrated, Responsive Supply Chain

Process Overview

In the chapters above the need for close interaction throughout the supply chain has become evident when discussing Fast Fashion. Zara's business model is distinguished - compared to other models - by a high degree of vertical integration, which integrates three consistently customer-oriented value-added processes of the fashion business: "Design/ Production", "Logistics", and "Store". The section "Design/Production" includes trend identification and collection development as well as the textile and clothing production. "Logistics" include bundling and the subsequent distribution of the goods centrally from a logistics platform. The section "Store" especially includes PoS marketing, presentation of stock, sale and advertising (mainly sales room formation and shop window advertise-ment). The surrounding section "teams" includes the employees with their different functions in the various value-added processes.[119]

The model has a flexible, integrated structure and has a strong customer focus on all value-added processes. The company's philosophy is: "Creativity, quality design and rapid turnaround to adjust to changing market demands." Insofar, the success of Zara is not accounted for by the single value-added functions - It is founded in an optimized, responsive supply chain, which has a strong customer focus and enables the company to design, produce and deliver new clothing in stores worldwide within 15 days. Such a velocity has benchmark character in the branch in which designers often need months to plan collections. And this is referred to as Fast Fashion.[120] According to that, Zara's supply chain strategy can be described as a concept that combines agility and leanness. It follows a Leagile Supply Chain strategy.[121]

---

[116] Cf. Zentes (2012), p. 702
[117] Cf. Tagesspiegel (2012): Im Reich der Zaras, p. 2
[118] Cf. Forbes (2015): Zara Leads in Fast Fashion, p. 1
[119] Cf. Zentes (2012), p. 701
[120] Cf. Zentes (2012), p. 702
[121] Cf. Zentes (2012), p. 709

Since Zara can offer the latest fashion so quickly, about 80 to 85% of the full selling prices are taken. The industry average is about 60 to 70%. In addition, a substantial advantage results from correspondingly higher margins, as no middlemen are interposed. The rapid identification of new design trends and developments, their processing and marketing as well as the response to the own sales data and customer needs, form an innovative process.[122] So far Zara realized both a forecasting of trends and a reactive policy of postponement. As a result, the production decisions are postponed as long as possible in order to meet the customer's taste as precisely as possible. Moreover, six months before a season starts Zara sets only 15 to 25% of the production, while there is an industry average of about 45 to 60%.[123] This responsiveness and the postponement of decisions until trends become known allow Zara to reduce inventories and forcast error.[124]

Design and Production as a Business Process

The design teams create all models of the campaigns. Thereby, not only the prevailing fashion trends, but also the information received from customers in the stores (sales data and customer requests) serve as inspirations for new collections. A nonstop flow of data from stores conveys the costumer's desires and demands. It helps to give shape to the ideas, trends, and tastes developing in the world.[125] The analysis and evaluations of sales data is performed daily in each store, and forwarded directly to the headquarters with the help of modern technologies. Thus, the information loop between the consumer and the upstream processes is closed.

The success of the collections lies in the ability to identify and implement the continuously changing fashion trends. Thus, new models can be adapted to the customer's wishes. Inditex uses the flexibility of its business model to accommodate potential, occurring trend changes in the course of fashion campaigns and to meet these changes with new product offerings as soon as possible. Every year, the designers create more than 40,000 models, of which approximately 10,000 models are selected for production. The patterns are designed digitally and sent promptly to the suppliers and production centers. In this context, design is understood as a fully integrated process within the supply chain.[126]

Furthermore, Zara devided the three-month sale season (for each of fall, winter, spring, and summer) into three 1-month periods. In the first month, the companies decide on quantities without knowing what sales would be like. For the second month, after observing the first week of demand, Zara makes its production decisions. In the third month, after observing the

---

[122] Cf. Zentes (2012), p. 702
[123] Cf. Hines (2007), p. 45
[124] Cf. Chopra (2013), p. 26
[125] Cf. Bermann (2013), p. 383
[126] Cf. Zentes (2012), p. 703

entire first month of sales, Zara makes its production decisions. Quick response allows Zara to respond to trends rather than having to predict them.[127]

The key element of this process forms the Point of Sale. This means, that the stores with carefully designed showrooms - in which the customers should feel comfortable as they discover the offered fashion - serve to gather the necessary information to adjust supply to demand. The deciding factor in this model is the ability to adapt the offer to customer wishes in the shortest possible time. Thus, at least some parts of the collection with a high fashion share are refered to design-on-demand retailing - the immediate adaptation to individual customer requirements.

In this connection, the modern and trend led collections with rapid adaptation of customer requirements on the basis of high delivery speeds, support the positioning as an en vogue quality experience brand. For this, the couture cuts of renowned designers, such as Prada or Gucci, are adapted. Trendscouts sift through fashion shows, fairs, social events or nightclubs worldwide. Partly Zara even gets ahead of haute couture designers, but this has to be at a much lower price with correspondingly less expensive and lower quality materials.[128]

Inditex has developed a flexible procurement and production system. Zara produces the goods mostly by itself. So, Zara can react quickly to trends and deliver products when they are needed (just-in-time). Storage costs and the dependence on producers are minimized.[129] While other manufacturers entirely outsource their production in low-wage countries, Zara submits 40% of the materials from the group's own holdings, 60% are supplied from closely connected suppliers.[130] Zara has 1625 suppliers worldwide.[131] The production by geographic region is as follows: 52% of the goods are produced in geographical proximity to the headquarter in Spain, Portugal, Morocco and neighboring countries, 27% in Asia, 18% in the rest of Europe and 4% in other regions of the world.[132] Zara's production facilities in Asia focus on low costs and primarily produce standardized, low-value products that are sold in large amounts. The European facilities focus on being responsive and primarily produce cutting-edge designs whose demand is unpredictable. This combination of facilities allows the company to produce a wide variety of products in the most profitable manner.[133] It is a network of 400 specialized subcontractors, mostly small workshops near the headquarters. However, Inditex itself does the design, cutting and finishing processes. Easier styles are

---

[127] Cf. Chopra (2013), p. 389 f.
[128] Cf. Zentes (2012), p. 703
[129] Cf. Zentes (2012), p. 704
[130] Cf. Hines (2007), p. 45
[131] Cf. Textilwirtschaft (2015): Das Ringen der Riesen, p. 22
[132] Cf. Zentes (2012), p. 704
[133] Cf. Chopra (2013), p. 122

outsourced. In many cases, Inditex provided most of the fabrics and other required garments elements for the external suppliers.[134]

Regarding the Inditex production, costs are not the decisive factor to be competitive. Zara's production costs, for example, are 15% higher than for similar products of competitors. Zara has begun to produce in large quantities after the product has proven to be sellable at the PoS. First of all, Zara produces and presents very limited volumes of new items in certain key stores in order to assess the demand structure and to create exclusivity. They are produced on a larger scale only if consumer reactions were unam-biguously positive. This means that the product shortage attracts the customer's attention and stimulates immediate buying decisions. Scheduled out-of-stock situations promote sales. Overall, Inditex has a high success control of the entire supply chain - from the initial design of the designer to the delivery to stores. Due to the high proportion of just-in-time production, inventory costs and stock levels are reduced to a minimum.[135]

Distribution and Logistics Processes

To begin with the entire production, regardless of the country of origin, is deliverd to the central logistics centers. There the products are checked for quality standards and labeled with an international price tag. Afterwards, the products are delivered to all stores in short, regular intervals. Hundreds of thousands of garments leave the four logistics centers of Zara every day. Even the first logistics center already ensures an almost fully automated distribution to the different Zara stores. It has an area of about 280,000 square meters and is equipped with modern technologies that are specially adapted to Zara's logistic activities.[136] The products can be destributed throughout Europe by truck within 24 hours. The remaining locations (particularly overseas) are supplied by air within about 48 hours. This ensures that every Zara store gets new products twice a week. Principally, new stock is delivered with every shipment to afford a continuous renewal of the offer in the stores.[137]

Logistics and distribution take place in a tight, precisely timed planning. When ordering and receiving goods all parties must abide by a precisely defined time window. The verticalization in conjunction with efficient logisitics enables to respond quickly to market demand and to produce and deliver just-in-time.[138]

---

[134] Cf. Zentes (2012), p. 704
[135] Cf. Zentes (2012), p. 705
[136] Cf. Zentes (2012), p. 705
[137] Cf. Chopra (2013), p. 26 f.
[138] Cf. Zentes (2012), p. 705

Trading as a Business Process

The store does not constitute the final point of the process. It marks a new beginning of the process. It acts as a collection point for information about the market situation, which gives the design team new ideas and insights of trend changes in customer demand.

While other apparel companies use about 3.5% of its turnovers for advertising purposes, Inditex uses only 2% of this area. Special attention is paid to the design of the stores, both indoor and outdoor. A crucial role plays the attractiveness of the shop window decoration. The significance of shop windows is even more obvious, as showcases are regularly built in original size with special lighting in the corporate office. For example, the effect of day and night light can be analyzed there.[139] When designing the interior, the aim is to create a transparent area in which the clothing plays a major role and all barriers between garments and customers are eliminated.

The development strategy of Inditex' sales brands is the integration of its own sales outlets - that means, of stores which are managed by wholly or majority Inditex-owned companies. As shown, this applies to about 90% of Zara-owned stores. In markets with low sales potential or cultural differences, the group has expanded its branch network through franchising agreements with local leading retail companies. Due to that, Inditex achieved a largely centralized management and a global image to international customers.[140]

5.2.2. Key Processes of the Supply Chain Management

As clarified, Zara developed a highly efficient supply chain as a central competitive advantage. The essential characteristics of supply chain management can be summarized as follows:

- Maximum Speed
- Enhanced Design
- Vertical Integration
- Uninhibited Flow of Information
- Modern IT Systems
- Optimized Flow of Goods
- Investments in Processes rather than in Advertising and Price Reductions.

---

[139] Cf. Zentes (2012), p. 705
[140] Cf. Zentes (2012), p. 706

Maximum Speed

"Speed" is the central characteristic of Fast Fashion retailers. Zara has significantly influenced this strategic group by the optimization of its supply chain.[141] As a result of this optimization Zara, as emphasized, ensures that a garment passes the whole process chain from design to production, delivery, and availability in one of the stores from all over the world within 15 days.[142] Meanwhile, competitors have lead times that range from three to nine months.[143] The company also supplies its stores twice a week with textiles and once a week with shoes, this guarantees new goods at every delivery.[144]

Controlled and Enhanced Design

As the high speed and short lead times have priority in Zara's value creation process, the strict controls are expanding on the design too. Zara deliberately does not recruit famous designers, but relies on young upcoming designers who usually come directly from university. The degree of creativity in Zara's design department is constrained by tight set parameters that result from efficiency and speed aspects. Thus, as an example, there is only a minimal number of patterns available for the designer. Due to time and cost reasons, Zara only makes use of existing material for required fabrics, yarns and cloths. The advantage of this procedure is that the production process must not be interrupted, because of not having to wait for the delivery of components.[145]

Further, Enhanced Design is a key part of Zara's design strategy. It concentrates on product development and is about improved design efforts that result in a marginal increase to consumer value. Enhanced Design also results in a more popular product and hence greater market share or size.[146] Enhanced Design describes the production of very fashionable products, which increase the costumer's value and makes them willing to pay full price. Zara aims to accelerate fashion-cycles, frequently bringing the latest products to the market by using Enhanced Design.[147]

Vertical Integration

Vertical integration means that the business processes are organized across the value chain and that the classic division of tasks between production and trade is resolved. Zara has developed from a mere textile producer to a vertically integrated textile company. It takes a lot of the sales and procurement added value functions itself.

---

[141] Cf. Zentes (2012), p. 706
[142] For further Information: Cf. Zentes (2012), Abb. 5.68, p. 706
[143] Cf. Chopra (2013), p. 389
[144] Cf. Zentes (2012), p. 706
[145] Cf. Zentes (2012), p. 706
[146] Cf. Cachon (2011), p. 784 f.
[147] For further Information: Cf. Choi (2014), p. 31

Relative to the conventional practice in the fashion trade, Zara has not outsourced a large part of the production. It is rather kept in-house. Investments in capital assets owe Zara an increased flexibility and control over the production schedules and capacities. At the same time, a high level of dependency from external suppliers is prevented. The automated just-in-time systems are demanding. Other functions with outsourcing potential, such as warehousing and distribution, are also carried out within the company's logistics centers. Both are often underused and - as in the factories - the maximization of the economies of scale does not have priority. Free capacities should rather be "reserved" in order to respond quickly to unforeseen demand and in peak located demand.[148]

Uninhibited Flow of Information

Basic prerequisite for the functioning of the business model is the immediate and comprehensive exchange of information between all actors in the supply chain. Therefore, the organizational structures and work processes are geared through targeted reduction of bureaucracy to facilitating the flow of information between customers, store managers, designers, production staff, warehouse managers, and distributors. To promote rapid and direct communication, Zara keeps the three sections for men, women, and children's clothing separate - although this means extra costs or expenses are not optimized by the non-use of possible synergy effects.[149] The company believes that the retention of three parallel operating channels with own procurement, own production planning, own design, and own distribution enables a more flexible control of the supply chain.

To ensure an optimal exchange of information between designers, market specialists and procurement and production planners, the members of these three functional groups are located in close proximity. This facilitates the formation of cross-functional teams. There-fore, the speed and quality of the design process has substantially increased.[150]

Modern IT Systems

The exchange of information is considerably promoted by the use of modern IT systems. In the communication between store managers and market specialists, Personal Digital Assistants (PDA) are increasingly used to identify both orders and sales figures as well as customer opinions and rumors of new fashion trends. The designers work with computer-aided design (CAD) systems in which they can make the "fine-tuning", e. g. regarding the colors, and in which the information can be passed to specific machines in the factories in

---

[148] Cf. Zentes (2012), p. 707
[149] Cf. Zentes (2012), p. 707
[150] Cf. Zentes (2012), p. 708

real time. The movements of particular pieces of fabric, that must be joined together to form a garment, can be tracked using barcodes through the entire production process.[151]

Moreover, Zara's planning and information systems allow store managers to track demand to schedule sales staff to work at peak times, in line with costumer and sales trends. Furthermore, store managers also use handheld computers that immediately rank garments by sales, so that they can reorder bestsellers immediatly. This provides a significant competive advantage for Zara over its Fast Fashion rivals.[152]

Due to the data update and the vertical integration, Zara succeeds to mitigate the so-called "bullwhip effect". This means that small deviations, for example of order quantities, tend to enlarge as they pass through the supply chain. Thus, a small order quantity can substantially enlarge by further transmission operations - from wholesale to the supplier and where appropriate, to the presuppliers. The variability of the demand rises increasingly, the further one moves along the supply chain. A vertical company equipped with the latest IT infrastructure like Zara can minimize this disadvantageous effect through ongoing data updating and transmission.[153]

Optimized Flow of Goods

Beside the flow of information, the flow of goods is also planned exactly in advance. The successive steps in the process chain are tightly scheduled and coordinated almost synchronously with one another. Therefore, every store manager receives specifically defined, mandatory time frames for order placement twice a week. The „order fulfillment" as the next sub-process proceeds equally - is precisely planned and reliable. The ordered goods are prepared at the distribution center overnight and usually delivered by truck or aeroplane. The exact time of arrival of the goods can be accurately predicted from the store manager, as the scheduled delivery time is adhered. In Europe, delivery is usually within 24 hours, and outside Europe for outlets in America and Asia about 48 hours. The goods can be sorted in the sales area immediately upon their arrival, as they are already priced when delivered presentation-ready.[154]

Investments in Processes rather than in Advertising and Price Reductions

For Zara, the fast timing of processes and synchronization are of particular importance. Therefore, financial resources are invested in all areas that contribute to increase the reaction rate, flexibility and efficiency of the supply chain as a whole. Zara has made substantial capital investments in its production and distribution capacity and uses this

---

[151] Cf. Zentes (2012), p. 708
[152] Cf. Chopra (2012), p. 64
[153] Cf. Zentes (2012), p. 708
[154] Cf. Zentes (2012), p. 708

against the backdrop of consistent customer orientation.[155] Moreover, Zara also invests heavily in information technology to ensure that the latest sales data is available to drive replenishment and production decisions.[156]

As indicated, a large part of the investments of Zara is for supply chain processes to achieve their optimization by reducing the lead times. The company invests only 2% of its turnover in advertising.[157] Not having advertising is an imperturbable part of the business model.[158] This means that the shop windows and store decorations function as the primary communication media. The avoidance of price reductions has already been pointed out in the previous chapters.[159]

5.2.3. Conclusion

Zara's supply chain can be characterized as market sensitive, as it is reminiscent of measures of Quick Response in the fashion industry, for example, by the direct trans-mission of PoS data via Electronic Data Interchange (EDI) and responsiveness to actual demand, although it also operates forecast oriented. Through integrative and cooperative exchange of information, supply chain partner processes are integrated so that a network-like structure emerges.[160]

The vertical integration and the design-on-demand or Quick Response form the key success factors through which Zara is able to implement current trends and customer requirements. Here it becomes clear that individual interfaces or processes are not optimized, but the supply chain as a whole is configured. An image transfer in the entire collection and an Unique Selling Proposition (USP) in the market result from the benefits generated in this way. As a consequence, short-term successes arise, as there are achievable higher selling prices, sales growth, and despite higher costs even a profit growth. In the long term, the USP is in Zara's business model, which is very difficult to copy. Considering this basis, Zara picks out the "speed" factor even in the corporate growth. Zara plans to move into the Australian and South African market with a stationary business and the US and Japanese market with online business.[161] Further, Zara plans a huge expansion in the next year: They plan to open 320 to 400 new stores.[162] Moreover, Zara defined a strategic plan from 2014 to 2018 to foster a stable and sustainable supply chain.[163] Thus, they want to secure supply chain management tools and build innovative and collaborative programmes for their

---

[155] Cf. Zentes (2012), p. 710
[156] Cf. Chopra (2013), p. 26
[157] Cf. Zentes (2012), p. 709
[158] Cf. Textilwirtschaft (2015): Das Ringen der Riesen, p. 20
[159] Cf. Zentes (2012), p. 709
[160] Cf. Zentes (2012), p. 709
[161] Cf. Zentes (2012), p. 710
[162] Cf. Textilwirtschaft (2013): Das Ringen der Riesen, p. 22
[163] For further Information: Cf. Inditex Annual Report (2013), p. 53

sustainability.[164] It will be interesting to observe how Zara will continue its revolutionary and international development from an organiza-tional and competitive strategical point of view.

6. Conclusion

In summary it can be said that there are three main fashion specific supply chain challenges: Swift Perishability, Uncertain Demand, and Long Lead Times.

These can be approached using the concept of Fast Fashion. In the main, it represents agilty and responsiveness.[165] Furthermore, it encompasses manufacturing near the markets and unrestrained flow of information.[166] In general, it is aimed at optimizing the supply chain in order to design and manufacture quickly.[167]

The example of the Spanish clothing retailer Zara showed, that the concept of Fast Fashion emphasizes - not only in theory but also in practice - a promising supply chain strategy.[168] Zara's business model characterized by enhanced design, vertical integration, uninhibited flow of information, optimized flow of goods, modern IT systems, and investments in processes[169] Thereby, Quick Response allows Zara to respond to trends rapidly. Zara's main advantage is to be vertically integrated into responsive manufacturing and retailing. Due to this, Zara has become one of the largest Fast Fashion retailers with high profits.[170]

Nevertheless, it is recommended to do further research to clarify how the realization of the Fast Fashion concept brings benefit to a fashion retailer - for example within profit increase. Moreover, it is important to take a closer look on presuppositions, potential hazards and risks, and the financial impact of the implementation of Fast Fashion. A final conlusion about Fast Fashion's suitability to approach the fashion specific supply chain challenges will only be possible by a review of the aforementioned aspects.

---

[164] Cf. Inditex Annual Report (2013), p. 51
[165] Cf. Diruf (2007), p. 6
[166] Cf. Chopra (2013), p. 65
[167] Cf. Textilwirtschaft (2013): Das Ringen der Riesen, p. 20 ff.
[168] Cf. Forbes (2015): Zara Leads in Fast Fashion, p. 1
[169] Cf. Zentes (2012), p. 706
[170] Cf. Chopra (2013), p. 390

7. List of References

1. Literature

Barnes, L.; Lea-Greenwood, G. (2006): Fashion Marketing and Fashion Management,
10. Edt., Manchester 2006

Berman, B.; Evans, J. R. (2013): Retail Management – A Strategic Approach,
12. Etd., London 2013

Diruf, G. (2007): Nutzung agiler Produktionsprozesse in Supply Chains für Modeprodukte,
3271. Edt., Frankfurt am Main 2007

Choi, T.-M. (2014): Fast Fashion Systems: Theories and Applications,
1. Edt., London 2014

Chopra, S.; Meindl, P. (2013): Supply Chain Management - Strategy, Planning and Operation,
5. Edt., Essex 2013

Donnellan, J. (2014): Merchandise Buying and Management,
4. Edt., London 2014

Draft, R.; Kendrick, M.; Vershinina, N. (2010): Mangement,
9. Edt., Hampshire 2010

Easey, M. (2009): Fashion Marketing,
4. Edt., Oxford 2009

Fernie, J.; Sparks, L. (2014): Logistics and Retail Management,
4. Edt., London 2014

Hertel, J.; Zentes, J.; Schramm-Klein, H. (2011): Supply-Chain-Management und Warenwirtschaftssysteme im Handel,
2. Edt., Berlin Heidelberg 2011

Hines, T.; Bruce, M. (2007): Fashion marketing - Contemporary Issues,
2. Edt., Burlington 2007

Jackson, T,; Shaw, D. (2006): The Fashion Handbook,

    1. Edt., Abingdon 2006

Lamb, C.; Hair, J.; McDaniel, C. (2010): Marketing,

    11. Edt., Mason 2010

Liebmann, H.-P.; Zentes, J.; Swoboda, B. (2008): Handelsmanagement,

    2. Edt., München 2008

Porter, M. (2010): Wettbewerbsvorteile – Spitzenleistung erreichen und behaupten,

    7. Edt., Frankfurt 2010

Tandler, S. (2013): Supply Chain Safety Management,

    1. Edt., Wiesbaden 2013

Werner, H. (2013): Supply Chain Management – Grundlagen, Strategien, Instrumente und Controlling,

    5. Edt., Wiesbaden 2013

Zentes, J.; Swoboda, B. (2011): Fallstudien zum Internationalen Management,

    4. Edt., Wiesbaden 2011

Zentes, J.; Swoboda, B. (2012): Handelsmanagement,

    3. Edt., München 2012

2. Internet Sources

N. U. (2015): Bossard Proven Productivity, Supply Chain Management - Challenges and Solutions

    http://www.bossard.com/en/how-we-add-value/key-challenges-in-supply-chain-management.aspx

    Date of Impression: 22.07.2015

N. U. (2015): Canadian Supply Chain Sector Council, Supply Chain Definitions

    http://www.supplychaincanada.org/en/supply-chain

    Date of Impression: 21.07.2015

Loeb, W. (2015): Forbes, Zara Leads in Fast Fashion

    http://www.forbes.com/sites/walterloeb/2015/03/30/zara-leads-in-fast-fashion/

    Date of Impression: 11.05.2015

Swartz, S. (N. D.): Inbound Logisitics, Challenges for Today's Global Supply Chain

    http://www.inboundlogistics.com/cms/article/challenges-for-todays-global-supply-

chain-cost-profitability-and-personalization/
Date of Impression: 22.07.2015

N. U. (2015): Inditex, Zara
http://www.inditex.com/en/brands/zara
Date of Impression: 23.07.2015

N. U. (2015): Inditex, Inditex at a Glance
http://www.inditex.com/en/our_group/at_glance
Date of Impression: 23.07.2015

N. U. (2015): Inditex, Our History
http://www.inditex.com/en/our_group/our_history
Date of Impression: 23.07.2015

N. U. (N. D.): Lexikon der Nachhaltigkeit, Fast Fashion
https://www.nachhaltigkeit.info/artikel/fast_fashion_definition_2012.htm
Date of Impression: 11.07.2015

Wolf, P. (2012): Tagesspiegel, Im Reich der Zaras
http://www.tagesspiegel.de/wirtschaft/im-reich-der-zaras/6253900.html
Date of Impression: 23.07.2015

Kiron, M. (N. D.): Textile Learner, Fashion Cycle – Steps of Fashion Cycles
http://textilelearner.blogspot.de/2012/09/fashion-cycle-steps-of-fashion-cycles.html
Date of Impression: 20.07.2015

3. Other Sources

Cachon, G.; Swinney, R. (2011): Management Science, The Value of Fast Fashion: Quick Response, Enhanced Design and Strategic Consumer Behavior
Vol. 57, No. 4 2011

Landowski, K. (2015): Panorama Magazine, Höchstgeschwindigkeit
Berlin 2015

Nowicki, J. (2013): Textilwirtschaft, Das Ringen der Riesen
No. 32, 2013

N. U. (2013): Inditex Group, Annual Report 2013